Bullets in the Jewelry Box

by

Amy Riddell

FutureCycle Press
www.futurecycle.org

Bullets in the Jewelry Box

Published by FutureCycle Press
Mineral Bluff, Georgia, U.S.A.

ISBN: 978-0-9839985-2-5

Jon

Contents

Father Sends His Combat Medals in a Padded Brown Mailer, 1988

Like Janus, I look forward and back.
Twenty, thirty years gone,
Father earned these medals.
He was a soldier then.
Ten years on, he will become a felon.
From here, I can't make out the details yet,
the handcuffs and prisoner number from the DOC,
can't quite read all four counts: attempted murder
in the second degree, kidnapping
with a firearm, attempted sexual battery,
and aggravated assault.
Janus, the god of gates and doors
shows us how to change, that we can and must.
From the brown mailer, I pull nine medals
that would weigh heavy on me if I pinned them
to my blouse. Instead, I turn each tarnished coin
and examine both sides, front and back.

Part One

a girl is born
like a little bird opening its wing

The Word for Broken

Nothing left but the naming,
that ancient task.
If I reached back,
would I find the root
of our undoing,
the word for what
broke us, broken,
the isolated phonemes
sounding out what we
could never point to,
syllables pricking my throat?

I couldn't know the naming
would consume me,
my hunger as foreign
as any language, like him,
the source of grief, Father,
speaking the king's English,
his nouns and pronouns
piercing my silence.

Forsaking Our Pearls

Was I made in darkness?
Were the lights off or on?
Yes, it matters.

⌘

My mother loved me.
She was so beautiful,
my eclipse,
ornamental and dutiful,
blonde spit curl.
But my father made me
his favorite.
I can't say why.
I can only be sorry.
We were his children,
my sisters and I,
silent oysters
forsaking our pearls.

⌘

It is true I loved him;
I took his word,
but we made mistakes,
one born too early,
the other too late;
only I arrived on time,
but with the perfect will
to speak. Allegiance
put my sweet voice
to sleep.

Dislocation

We drove in silence
across the Sonoran,
last leg to Camp Pendleton
from Camp LeJeune.
In the Chevy's back seat,
my sleeping sisters slumped
beside me. Up front
in dash-lit darkness,
Mother stared ahead.
Father sucked on his cigar,
the lit end glowing red.

In His Grip

Our father sits mute before the six o'clock news.
He doesn't notice my sisters or me, looks up
only to watch our mother move across linoleum,
gets up only to reach for her. She becomes
breasts, thighs, hips—luckless in his grip.
We watch with our small eyes and crave
his touch, hungry as we are to be defined.
He never speaks—not even to utter her name
as she silently turns her face away from us.

Portrait of Father Eating Ice Cream While Watching the Evening News, 1970

Straight from the carton,
relaxed in his chair,
spoonful by spoonful
into his mouth. Towel draped
across his lap.

Dagger, machete,
pick concealed
in leather crop. What he
loves, all there—trophies
from Korea, Vietnam.
His wars. Across the room
I sit and watch him bring
the spoon around.
Vanilla drips.
TV flits and flickers.
He licks
and licks.

What I Thought

I was seven
when I thought a witch
had stolen my mother
while I was away
at camp.
I thought the witch
had buried my real mother
in the garden,
but I was mistaken
because we didn't have a garden
and the story was from
a book I had read.
At camp
counselors told us stories
in the dark around fires,
and my mind cantered away
from me. They said
Indians would attack,
so when a man
with an arrow through his heart
galloped up on a Shetland pony,
I cried
even though the arrow
wasn't real and the blood
was only grape juice.

Dead Man's Float

When I was twelve my father taught me
what to do if ever caught in an undertow.

If you can, he said, *swim parallel to shore.*
If not, let the current take you.

I stood chest deep in the Gulf of Mexico
and watched him demonstrate. *Don't fight,*

he said as he put his face in, letting his arms and legs
dangle until only his back bobbed in the smaller waves.

There were other lessons, too: how to drive a stick, lance
a boil, order whiskey neat. Not such useless things.

Love can move like a current—easy sometimes,
other times rough.

He led me into dangerous water,
his calm surface a trick

to make me think his love safe. His rip
stirred beneath. No escape, just the bargaining:

either the parallel swim that can't outpace
the undertow's reach or the dead man's float,

a pretend death with breath held and head submerged,
a bobbing half-life lived adrift in his love's pull.

A Taste of Ashes

The field burns after dark.
Father tends the fire
with shovel and broom.
Mother calls us girls away,
but he calls us back again.
He says new roots
need warmth, the underbrush
a blanket of ash.

Life drops to bare knees
in the yard. My sisters stumble
and fall. I dig remnants
of broken dishware from dirt,
his orders, so the horses won't cut
hooves. He ignores the sharp edge
in my eyes, beckons me into
the flames and shows me
the exact place to stand
while he sets fire to another
patch of weeds,
another stump.

Shopping List

It was the loaves of Wonder
bread, spears
of Vlasic pickles, the list
as long as one of Mama's
naps and the hour's drive
each way, alone,
in the silver-grey Chevrolet.

Fleishmann's stick
margarine, nine pounds
of ground round,
ten links of pepperoni, sliced,
and six bricks of cheddar.
It was Mama's signed check
in my pocket, the amount
to be filled in, the Vienna sausages
and the French-cut green beans.

It was the rutabaga's hard body
and the eggplant's soft.
The frozen okra
and the yellow squash.
It was heads of iceberg
lettuce to squeeze,
packages of frozen turnips
and black-eyed peas.
It was my learner's
permit and the long drive back,
the bags to carry in when
I got there, and the chicken
to cut up and fry after that.

Passenger

People are shit,
my father's words
repeated every day
on the road to school.
Forty-five minutes
he'd go on and on.
Barbed wire
out my window.

Always the same.
Hunched over the wheel,
Mother fuckers. Winter,
fall—didn't matter.
His eyes drained
of their blue.

Out my window,
live oaks cast shadows.
Black gum trees
stood dark. I shrank
against rough
upholstery. Orange
speedometer, the only
color.

Cars lined up behind.
The two-lane stretched on.
All the way
I said nothing,
went nowhere
but down,
down, down.

Where I Have Been

The body holds itself shut, refuses
all touch, sweats through dreams,
and wakes me. I want to see
but have no way down into my eyes,
what I have known, buried.

I sit at a small table
I can't reach across. No touch but his.
Hands folded, eyes closed,
I am his good girl. I want
to remember, but the opening
is so hard. The act of opening my eyes,
my hands so hard, and my mouth, I won't.
Don't ask.
It's too small for that.

I have no secret tunnel,
valved voices to open me,

only the stalled, mined, static flash:
my body kneeling on the carpet,
his pale calves and thighs before me,
and the other thing.

My Mother Speaks in Mother Tongue

I. Truth

I was thinking about the names of things
and how they carry what is known.
But here is a lie:

I married young and had three daughters.
When they were babies,
I bathed them in the kitchen sink.
You can't know my fear each time I lifted one
wet and slippery and red-faced.

I dressed those babies and fed them
and carried them until my back ached.
Wasn't I a good mother?

Is any of this true?

I know the names of things and their definitions
but not the connections.
I am unreliable. I lie.
But where is the truth? Is it the chair I sit in
and the way its shape holds me?

I married young and had three daughters.
When they were babies, I bathed them
in the kitchen sink. I loved them, I did.

II. Joy

> After Lucille Clifton

My girl was right.
Sorrow lives inside her,
a dry little body with a voice that begs
for water, for drink.
She has no tears.

She sees the cooking pot on my stove,
the hand I have for holding

a spoon, a lid;
The steam to dampen my eyes
she can see.

My face is in her face,
grey circles under brown eyes.
She cannot know what I know,
the unlikely connection:
that time when her body drank from mine.
What ocean does she grieve?
She begs for water, for drink
but has no tears.
Recriminations turn and burn
within me like fear.

III. Confession

Let me say I never held my girl
against her will

in the circle of my arms
in rooms made dark

with shades pulled down
against sun. She never wanted to run

away from me, from my tears and pleas
to please, please
explain once and for all why I cry
and what I fear. No, no!

My hands never gripped her shirt
and I never, ever hurt

her even a little. She never shook
or cried or even asked me to look
beyond myself to see her there,
fifteen years old

sitting in the dark, so cold
she shook and said nothing.

What Words

These words I make
mock spring's green lyric.
The dove out my window,
plump and able, perched
in a blossoming tree
and quietly cooing.
Not for me.

My singing hurts.
My logic aches.

But what words
can I make
to make
sense of?

Rough with Each Other

Lisa, remember those August days after school,
those hours waiting for Father, how we wrestled
in the cab of his truck and pulled
each other's hair, trying to twist
the other's will:

"I'll let go if you will."
      "You first."
            "No, you."

When Father finally showed,
he separated us with a single command:
"Sit on your hands."

My head ached the long drive home.
Palms sweaty beneath thighs, I sat trapped
in my own skin, between you and him. Lisa,

we traveled that road side by side.
Out the window, Martin's fields eased past.
Silent horses stood and grazed,
and roadside scripture claimed to show the way.

I know this now; I could have held
your hand. Could have. I didn't.

Blade at My Sister's Throat

"When the pin is pulled,
Mr. Grenade is not our friend."
                    —*U.S. Marine Corps Training Manual*

Who pulled our father's pin that day,
she didn't know.
Eighteen and moving out,
she had borrowed his truck—
was bringing it back. She walked
into his living room, didn't notice
him waiting by the TV,
hand behind his back.
But when she put the truck key
on the table, he was suddenly
there holding something sharp
against her throat. "Where have you been?"
His voice low, lips tight and white.
She didn't scream or even cry
but averted her eyes
and whispered, "I'm sorry."
He held her there and breathed
into her face the stink of coffee
and tobacco. "Bitch."
But his hand dropped, and she backed away,
out the door, down the walk,
into her car and a life
where every man along the way
could be hiding something
behind his back.

How It Goes On

Scrub-dirt past, sharpened ax, and Granny Dora pissing fast
down her legs while plowing. Just like a cow, you said, Mama.
Can I imagine? Your ma out back wringing biddies by the neck,
chopping heads and claws. She snatched you bald for nothing
much at all and slung you across the floor. There is more.

By lamplight, your brother couldn't make sense of work
the teacher sent home, so he held tight as your pa hit him
and hit him. Mama, see how I am what you need the most,
not a speechless ghost to cast out, but a daughter who will go
and has gone with you, offering flowers at those graves.
I have left so much unsaid, Mama, the bad light,
the lumpy bed, your sister balled up in a corner, afraid.

My sister balled up in a corner, afraid.

I know you can see how it goes on, Mama.

Interrogation

As if my father, the stalker, once said to me, "Girl,"
as if he said, "Girl," while overhead
a bare bulb lit the scene,
unblinking, blinding the room's shadows.
"Girly girl," as if binding my hands
and wagging one gloved finger under my nose.
"Tsk, tsk. Daddy always knows." As if he danced
from heel to toe and taped my mouth. "You are
my baby girl." His face wet with tears
as if he scrunched and posed.
"Oh my little girly girl, my crumb cake icing
doll, don't cry." As though he were lining
his instruments all in a row.

Burqa, the Right Word for Grief

Black shroud pulled on head to foot, the way to picture
grief's bald assumption about what can be endured

with hands fisted, fingers curled to submit, to abide
despair, that dry cup, and refuse even one sip to drink.

The throat suffers its raw ache, longs for what's been lost to simple
words now slipped inside the skin, inside silence where language
        lives.

Among the grieving and doomed, what can't be said must be kept
secret, like a woman shielded from the eyes of pitiless men.

Part Two

You do not do, you do not do
Any more, black shoe

Body of a Lunatic

The body can look like anything—
the blade a paring knife stabs
into an apple.
It can look like anything
and be what it is.

In the photograph, my father stands
shirtless on a white beach against
a backdrop of blue summer sky.
Sixty years old. His tanned chest
and shoulders are muscular.

He mugs for the camera,
his grey hair split by wind,
and reaches out his arms
as if to offer himself.

See, his note says,
*does this body look
like the body
of a lunatic?*

Whispers

Mother spends her nights watching TV, or she goes out.
"It takes my mind off things. I don't want to know
what your father is up to. I need distractions."

Father speaks in whispers,
says, "Cut life's throat,
feed on what you wound,
wound before you kill,
then eat your fill."

Mother calls and says, "Listen,
your father is at it again.
This time he went for his straight razor.
I'm not hurt but he probably needs stitches.
He won't go out. I thought someone ought to know."

I speak to fear, the gnawing
mouth inside my mouth,
his blood in my blood,
his voice in mine,
my tongue his meat.

"We were quietly eating breakfast like always.
Suddenly, your father leaned over and whispered a prayer.
'Let me be an instrument of peace,' he said, cutting a sausage
into neat little squares. I said nothing and gripped the edge
of my chair, waiting for his eyes to clear."

Threat

On a shelf in her closet,
Mother keeps the two bullets
in the jewelry box
where Father left them years ago
as a message for her
back when she lived with him
back when she wore the diamonds
and pearls he gave her. No note.
Just the bullets. One for her,
and one for him. She understood.

Subtext

Words crusted like cornbread
in the iron skillet. Nerves pulled taut.
Family dinners more than civil:
Please pass the gravy. No,
I wouldn't care for more black-eyed peas.

But in the jewelry box, the bullets,
hollow like *I love you*
and useless like so many promises—

I could never.

Dissolution

One day my father said,
"Look at this"
and pulled a photo
of a dead man
from a box he kept stored
in the den's built-ins.

Meanwhile,
in the driveway, my mother
sold a duvet cover,
the extra TV.
Tape holding up
the yard-sale sign
kept letting go its grip
and the sign would slip.
Downsizing again,
she was leaving behind
the house and my father,
divorcing him
for the third time.

Back inside,
my father held out
the photo. "See."
The man was Vietnamese.
I looked away.
"An informer I executed,"
Father said.
My concentration slipped.
Outside my mother
was still counting change.
"Sixty-four, sixty-five, sixty-six."

Another New Wife, 1996

While reading the newspaper one day,
Mother saw the wedding notice,
Father's newest wife, younger
than their youngest daughter.

The photo showed a bride in white veil
smiling at the camera, and behind her
a grey-haired man, my father,
in bow tie and tux. He smiled, too.

Over my mother's shoulder, a woman snorted
and said, "Look at that old man with that young girl.
Disgusting." Mother said nothing,
just folded the paper and tucked it in her purse.

One for Yes, Two for No

Mother said, "Keep your nose out of it."
Why get involved was her point.
To my thinking I was already involved,
being his daughter and all.
Maybe she'd been divorced from him
for twenty years and could overlook his
almost murdering a woman,

but his blood runs in my veins. "Fine,"
she said, "but if he finds out, you'll be sorry."
But *I* was thinking, *I'm already sorry.*
How much sorrier can I be?
Her point being, I could be a lot sorrier
if he got hold of me. Anyway,

if she didn't want me involved why
did she call at 6 a.m. to read the report
from the *Pensacola News*?
I didn't say that out loud, but I thought it.
I mean, if it's none of her business or mine,
why is she telling me? I can't remember

the exact headline, something like
"Woman Shot by Husband"
or "Man Arrested, Accused of Shooting Wife."
Or maybe it was "Woman Found Shot,
Near Death, Husband Accused."
I can't recall, but I do remember thinking,
"Well, good morning to you, too!" and
"God, I hope no one I know reads that."

Instead, I said, "Oh, shit."
And Mama said, *No shit.* And then *after*
I said maybe the police'd be interested to learn
what a handful he has always been, she said
"Keep your nose out of it." But there was no choice

what with his wife bleeding almost to death,
his holding her hostage, and her so weak,
the papers said, she couldn't speak
when police finally got there, had to squeeze
a detective's hand to answer questions—
one squeeze for *yes,* two for *no.*

After Mother and I Quarrel

She stands on her porch in a housecoat,
arms folded and face grim. I am backing out
the drive, looking behind myself, maneuvering
with one hand on the wheel and the other
waving goodbye out the window.

Daughter becomes the word
for being broken by the same weight.

Father's New Wife Survives and Testifies

(taken from court records of trial testimony)

"I covered my head
with my hands
and begged,
'Please don't.
Please don't.'
I jumped up
and ran and when
I got to the door, I
I remember, BAM,
falling backwards
against the louvers,
sliding down a little,
him right in my face
with a gun
and it going off
and not being
able to hear very well,
this strange look
on his face.
And then I fell
all the way down.
He grabbed my arm
and pulled me
into the other room.

I was thinking,
I am going to die.
I was on my back,
and he pushed my legs up
and got on top of me,
and I was crying then.

He asked questions and hit me
every time I didn't answer
fast enough.
The whole time

he kicked me
and hit me, he would say,
'Are you dead yet?'
I would open my eyes
and say, 'No.'
He'd say,
'What's wrong with you?
Why don't you die?'
Over and over,
'Why aren't you dead yet?
Why don't you die?
Do you want me
to finish you off?
Do you want
me to go ahead
and shoot you in the
head and finish
you off?'"

Confession

It is true—
I loved him.

Excerpt from Newspaper Report, 1998

"A 70-year-old retired Marine lieutenant colonel will spend the rest of his life in prison, but said during his sentencing . . . he still loved the wife he shot twice and tortured."

Portrait of Father Being Sentenced

As when the tightrope walker falters and then pilots his balance
in the same way that a boy who pretends to be an airplane
will dip and tilt his outstretched arms,
so too my father faltered, his composure lost
like a man paddling the air,
like a man reaching for a way to stand erect again,
shoulders back, above it all, chin lifted, the tilt of it
perfectly set as though he cradled a robin's egg
in its cleft, as though one slight tremble
of his lip would cast
a world to ruin.

Kisses

The day Father's sentence was read,
my sister phoned from court, crying:
thirty years—life for him at seventy.
She didn't know whether to be
happy or sad. As the bailiff
led him out, Father smiled
at her and blew kisses.

I remember kisses,
butterfly kisses on our cheeks.
Mother holding my face in her hands,
but our life not soft like the touch
of eyelashes on skin. Sometimes,
we had cotton candy and fireflies.
Sometimes, tree forts out back.
Milk cartons my mother cut in half
for me and spaghetti jars rinsed clean
to carry while I roamed the yard
for caterpillars and lizards.

Offerings

Father's gone to prison now.
I send no packages of caramels,
no cash for the commissary.
But as a child, I made offerings,
tins of sardines wrapped
for Father's Day. For Christmas,
a pipe and cherry tobacco.
I watched him pack the bowl,
watched how he lit it,
letting the flame burn
almost to his fingers.
He talked with pipe stem clenched
in his teeth, smoke billowing
from his mouth,
filling the space between us.

Contrition

My father, 73, pleads for release
July 6, 2000

"Dear Sir, I have brought upon myself
for the rest of my life the shame
and stigma of a convicted felon.
Nonetheless, in order to demonstrate
a contrite heart and my repentance,
and that obeying edicts
comes naturally to me,
I have, while behind bars,
on my own volition,
undertaken this provision
of my sentence: Anger
management. Until

well into my September years
I was a common, garden variety
ordinary person. But, in a moment
of madness, I became a felon.
But I swear to you as I swore
allegiance to my country—
never again! In August,
I will have served the three year
minimum mandatory part
of my sentence. I plead
that you release me
from prison, now, to stay
on probation for the
remainder of my life.
A respectful thank you.

Sincerely,

PS:
Please tell me if you
are going to release me

from prison. If not,
for my part,
decisions of great import
are a must."

Letter From Prison

My father writes the judge who sentenced him,
November 4, 2000

"Well, Sir, it's been three
years, and I've yet
to enjoy an erudite
discussion. This is a sad,
sad world of lost souls.

I am the eldest here.
This prison is awash
in homosexuals and child
molesters. As a 'civilian,'
I'd understood that these groups
did not fare well in prison. Not so,
they are accepted
without qualification.

Having dealt with numerous
nationalities and cultures,
I find no difficulty here
in that I treat everyone
in a courteous, gentlemanly
manner as I was reared
to do. I did, however, some
time ago 'endear'
myself to several guards
when I interceded on behalf
of a small, 40-plus year old
over the TV (which I don't watch).
I presented the sergeants with a note:
'In the interest of good
order and discipline it would be
well of you, the authority
figures, to delineate in writing
the procedures regarding TV use . . .'
and listed the here-to-fore

prisoner-agreed upon rules.
I assiduously avoid
the guards but felt compelled
in this case. I have been,
since, persona non grata.

One is put here as punishment
and as isolation, not to be further
punished a la constant inane harassment.
We are at the mercy
of the caprice of our keepers
who see us merely as objects.
Be that as it may,
our keepers cannot bother me. I'll not
lower myself to become upset
by their idiocy. Wednesday

when I was returning from the law
library, a guard threw a glob
of wet tissue at my feet.
'Take that with you,' he ordered. Without
a word, smiling to myself, I did,
depositing it in the next trash can.
I, truly, felt sorry for the poor soul—
what a horrible 'life'
he must live."

Minotaur Considered

For him, words are distant stars that prick light into darkness.
He has no stars, nor any words with which to say *because*
or *if only*. He can't say *maze* or *labyrinth*, can't speak
his longing, understands so little, is all blood and guts

and afternoon naps, growling in his sleep. Among the bones,
he can gnaw no light into the thing that he is, can't name
what he is, what the gods made remorseless
and uncomprehending, beyond redemption or love.

Lament

Hope bites the tongue
like the pomegranate's seed,
sweet pulp, bitter core.

Desire, that round and hairy kiwi,
rots in the crisper drawer.

The elements forget.
Wind drowses, water sleeps.
No fire speaks from the beggar's ashcan.

No birth from any blood.

Bluebeard's Daughter Ponders

Does he imagine us in graves, conjure
what is left, scraps of blouse and matted hair?
Does he think we owe him our
last minutes, each filled with what? Fear,

tears, maybe even prayers. His gun
they've taken. They've locked him away. A wish
can't unchain the life he lives now among men
like himself. Their lies are bitter ash

on tongues that have not a single word
to name what they are. We are victims,
too, his wife and daughters, who tried (but failed)
with soft kisses to turn him from his dreadful whims.

Do our voices murmur in his guiltless sleep?
Does he long for redemption. Does he ever weep?

Hide and Seek

Mother, have you woken from your sleep?
My body summons you. I need
to hear your voice singing:

"You can come out now!"

Can I come out now,
Can we come out now,

Can we all come on out,

you, Mother,
and your precious
little daughters?

Dream of Burial

A grave would be a place to visit at last
to curse, raise a fist,
kick a stone.

I am five years old on a rocky shore of the Pacific Ocean.
Father smiles up at me from the place
he has climbed down to.

Because I have asked him,
he returns my just-caught fish
to the sea.

Years later, he sits across from me, his latest bride
excused to the restroom,
and threatens,

"Don't tell her anything."

A grave would be a place of real dirt
where the earth might open
to receive the confusion I still carry.

I could bury him,
erect a stone, and put
all the grief to rest.

His Arms

When I was a girl my father spooned me
and sang a song.

My body misgave the embrace,
Father's onion scent. His voice,
unused to tender tones, gruff
in the bedtime quiet.
He always repeated the last line twice,
his arms holding me so tightly
I could catch only shallow breaths.

I let him sing to me and hold me.
I loved him as a child loves
and longed to have no fear.

While he held me, secrets
that I still can't know wormed
through his bitten core.

Those secrets hollowed us.

They crawled the remains
of our life, shredding
all our scrapbook smiles.

In the end, handcuffed
at the wrist, he stepped into court
like a sleep walker drowsed
by a tired song,
a song he sang long ago
while he held me
in his arms.

Part Three

Everyone in me is a bird.
I am beating all my wings.

When Love Had No Sun

Brad, I held your hand that night
as we walked through Tom's pasture.

The heavens shone
with stars even though

we were not yet in love,
or maybe I was.

In November cold,
you pulled me onto a blanket

of frost, whispering "Come here,"
like a wish coming true,

your mouth feeding
me promises.

Though that night made me older,
I was still young.

I didn't know yet that love could vanish
through a darkened bedroom window

or that it could reappear as casually
as morning sun, like you did,

tapping at the glass
and offering

a small bouquet of azaleas taken
from a neighbor's yard.

Days I couldn't find you anymore
were like mud on my skin,

no key under the mat,
your windows curtained.

You weren't there to feel the punch
of Demerol in the thigh

or to hear the doctor say,
This will hurt.

If only I'd imagined the stars
over Tom's pasture

as butterflies set free
from a jar

like those remembered
from childhood

when my body was mine alone,
then the wishes

inside me might still flicker,
their wings intact.

Seven Ways of Looking at a Butterfly

After Wallace Stevens

1

Within the purple blossom of the flowering Lantana
the only moving things
were the wings of a yellow butterfly.

2

My mind was folded into two parts
and spread open
like butterfly wings.

3

The butterfly floated among the falling autumn leaves,
caught up in a gust of wind that blew it away.

4

A dandelion and a breath of air
are one.
A dandelion, a breath of air, and a butterfly
are one.

5

I do not know which to prefer,
the serenity of opening
or the serenity of closing,
the butterfly in flight
or at rest among the blossoms of the bottlebrush tree.

6

Rain drops fell all day and filled the bird bath.
The shadow of the butterfly
crisscrossed the pool of water.
Grief rippled in the shadow.

7

Oh armed men of Afghanistan,
why do you hide in mountain caves
along the Pakistani border
and rain down bullets?
Do you not see how a child's kite
floats in the city sky like a butterfly?

Persephone Lost

Before the man snatched her,
she was like Persephone
picking daffodils on a hillside.
She was just a little girl
tending potted petunias outside the trailer
where she lived. She smelled of sweet
gardenias and of laundry line-dried
in the sun. After she was gone,
her grandmother, wild-eyed like Demeter,
searched and searched,
but neighbors watched out their windows
and the sun in this story was only the sun
and rose and set day after day
while grief choked the grandmother
and the earth held the girl's breathless
body. There was no magic, no grieving
goddess to shut everything down,
only her school clothes
folded there neatly in the chair,
set out at bedtime after Sunday night
church. Before death,
she thrashed about
in the garbage bag, realizing
that he had buried her.
Not wanting to be lost,
she scratched and clawed
for light and air, for life itself,
and, clawing, tore the bag
but there was no use. Weeks later,
when police found her,
the first thing they saw
poking through
like some trick of new
life sprouting in the dirt—
two little fingers.

Crocus

What is this purple
appetizer serving its color
from a green throat fed
by rain? Small spoon
for the eye,
meal of laughter,
ridiculous finger bowl,
grape, plump, oblong tear,
give me your joyous
juices bitten free,
your full belly,
your thimble full
of mercy.

Disarmed

Jon, we first met outdoors.
You sat tipped back in a chair,
Sporting News opened in your lap.
Sugar maples lit the courtyard.
A muted breeze blew my skirt.
The day was lovely but ordinary,
the moment ordinary, too, except
when I walked by, you looked up,
said "Hi," and your smile
stopped me, turned me even,
mid-step, one foot, then the other,
taking me back to you.

In Celebration

Jon, with you, I go
into dark caves.
I find shelter. We know the breathing
in bed and our
whispering in the dark.

We know the distance
between us.

When I am the faintest star
in the night sky, you are the restful
meadow, and when I am the meadow,
you are the star.

Love holds us
in the cosmos
in its tight cocoon.

Blue Moon Blessing

Emergency Caesarean: June 1, 1996

It was June,
a month of two full moons.

Epidural tubing threaded into my spine.

When they broke my water,
meconium, another word for distress,

stained the amniotic fluid.

Pitocin, pitocin, pitocin—
we rocked in that great green ocean.

At one after noon, the monitor lost her pulse,

hands cut me, pulled her to safety,
and blood washed over us.

A New Being

When they opened me,
every lamp was lit
to let the doctor see
where she grew
all those months,
the kindled embryo,
wholesome marvel.

A new being
with gentle hands,
I find her, take care
to tend her, keep busy
with tiny fingernails
to trim, clippers
to steady while I
snip translucent
slivers, hold
my mouth just so,
so as not to nick
tender fingertips.

When she sleeps, I roll
my husband's socks
and listen, my ear cocked,
all my lamps lit.

What I know of love,
my body taught
through muscled certainty
and the contractions'
relentless grip.
The lesson owns us,
her life a promise kept.
She suckles and grows
at my breast.
She flourishes even now
cradled in my arms.

Light through My Window

Journal open, pen resting nearby,
but my hands lie limp in my lap.
In the desk's black finish
no light bounces, nothing reflects.
My eyes see slatted shadows
the window blinds cast on these walls.
Morning light comes in.
The day begins this way.
If I don't reflect, thread the line of thought
onto the page, its bold embroidery
won't draw me back here again.
I will remain transfixed by the lines
crisscrossing my open palms
and the page before me on the desk
in the room filling with morning light.

This Morning

my daughter tramples
a square of sunlight
on the kitchen floor,
and shadows skip
out of her way—
eclipsing all sadness.

Limitation of Order

I hang my laundry in the sun—
shirt to sheet, sheet to spread—
collect my spoons in a single drawer.
My life depends on this.

I count the steps, sixteen,
from bath to kitchen, four more
to back door. This contains me:
wall, ceiling, floor.

What keeps me moving?
A pan of water set to boil,
shirts pinned to the line,
my child's cough? Yes.

Darkness borders
the laundry, the drawer,
the steps I take.
But I imagine the possibilities:

A room in disarray,
a bedroom corner
never swept, a gust of wind
that rifles papers on my desk.

Learning the Language of Need

My daughter has two words, just two,
One an interjection, the other a noun.

"Bye bye," she says, "bye bye."
This is a game we play.

"Baby," I say, "bye bye," and pretend
to go away. When she says, "Mama,"

I hear her. "Mama," she says,
and holds out her arms. I see her.

She needs me. "Mama, mama."
With her hands, she begs the air.

Julie Holds a Hummingbird

Julie holds her small hand
flat. The hummer,
no bigger than her finger,
sits quietly there. In flight
its wings beat
fifty-three times per second,
but now its brown body
is as still as a supplicant's,
wings and claws tucked,
the soft back silky
like a key-chain rabbit's foot
won at the fair. So still
but alive, too,
the heart pounding out
200 beats, turbulence masked
in feathered quietude. Its beak
a fragile twig,
useful for drawing forth the nectar,
sweet strength against
cold, against
death. The black eyes depthless,
no way in. White breast
a cotton ball soft
as breath. Julie holds
her own breath, her head bent
to get a closer look, the hummer
holding still, Julie finding
the way to be still, to hold
without closing her grip,
to stay this way, learning
to keep her hand open,
herself open
to the bird,
to this moment,
to whatever good
that comes.

In the Deep End

Poolside at bay drive pool, my back and shoulders rest
against a wicker chaise. Sun browns me.
Through the thick haze of half sleep, I hear
my thirteen-year-old daughter's persistent call.
Her need punches awake my other self,
the one who trims crusts from slices of bread
and hand-washes training bras
just to suit and please this child I love.

Sunlit drops sparkle on Julie's face.
Crepe myrtle petals carpet the concrete deck.
I put aside all things and root
in the pool bag to find what Julie wants.

Down in the shallow end,
a bare-faced mother stands hip deep
and squints against the sun.
She holds out her arms, and her toddler jumps in.
My daughter, a young woman now, waits
in the deep end. I go to her with the goggles.
How easily I can give her the thing she needs.

I recall nights her cry woke me.
We rocked together in pre-dawn darkness,
lullabies soothing our troubles, time slowing,
then creeping until finally it stopped,
lifting all fatigue and fear from those quiet hours.

She lifts her face now and smiles.
Then she's gone, swimming away from me,
down beneath the chlorine-clear surface lit
with sun and pink petals. She kicks
to take herself deeper, her body snaking
along the bottom, golden-blonde hair dark
and slick as rope. She's in deep now,
her eyes open to find what awaits her there.

Teaching my Daughter to Drive

After my daughter runs a red light,
she glances over at me with big eyes.

Learning to read the timing of traffic signals,
she sometimes slows down on the green,

stopping a car's length shy of the mark.
Other times, she accelerates on the yellow

and flies through at fifty. Either way,
I bite my words to crack them.

I grind and chew them into harmless bits
because I know how words can be stones.

Cinderella's Wrinkle

Let's say her happilyeverafter
was charmed
like that glass slipper,

her bridal finery boxed,

not a single stitch pulled
or a mouthful
moth-bitten.

Suppose all those years

sat on her lightly, gravity
misting her
like a spritz of perfume,

until one day in the mirror,

right in the center
of her never-knitted brow,
a wrinkle.

Imagine her mouth then,

puckered in concern,
no longer a hibiscus bloom.
Instead its *O* falters.

It wilts and sags.

Suppose she knows the midnight hour
is upon her, that the pumpkin's
been left to rot.

If the fairy godmother's magic

has finally been spent,
what's left to look forward to
but a dowager's hump?

Or she could say "So what?"

to the skin tag,
the jowl, and the hag's
hairy wart

and imagine herself

naked at a window,
the sun warming her skin,
her bare face lifted

and her gaze turned in.

Her wrinkle forgotten,
she could hum softly
and stroke

a lock of hair,

her hand mirror cracked
and gathering dust
on a shelf.

A New Connotation for Purple

Purple like a plum taken chilled
From the refrigerator and warmed
between my husband's hands.

Like the sky at dusk after a storm
has blown sweetgum leaves
across the yard.
Neighbor girls on bikes ride past.
Their laughter floats toward me
as I walk barefoot to check the mail
and find hand-written letters
from both my sisters.

By the fire, there are cups of tea,
the softest chair, and a cushioned stool
for my feet. On the sofa, my daughter naps
while my husband reads his *Atlantic*.

When I am weary, weary,
he will lead me to rest
in cool darkness, placing the pillow
and switching off the light.
Darkness will be the purple
not of bruises or bitter wine
but the color of the sweet grapes
my daughter offers.

Surrender

I am a woman who eases herself
into a bath, who dips
fingertips in first
to test the heat.
Under my breath, I sing
a lullaby,
spilling all the notes
into the water
which collects such things.

Bluebeard's Daughter

I collect light,
find a shaft here,
a shimmer there,
and fill my pockets.

I look everywhere—
in my husband's hands,
my daughter's smile—
and gather whatever I find,
even the TV's flicker.
I know to do this.

Though Father is locked away now,
I shape a window
through which I can see
beyond myself
and climb to safety.

When he led me
into the dark halls
of his misery and made me
the keeper of his keys,
the light nourished me

until the day came when
finally I opened my mouth
to speak and picked up my pen
to write and the light poured
from me and for that time

I became like the sun,
a star beyond darkness.

Notes

"Father's New Wife Survives and Testifies" is a found poem adapted from trial transcripts filed in the Circuit Court of Escambia County, Florida. The poem uses exact words from the testimony with some parts edited out.

"Contrition" and "Letter from Prison" are found poems. They use my father's actual words from letters that he wrote to Judge Terry Terrell, who presided over his trial and sentenced him. The letters, which have been edited here, are kept in my father's case file which is held in the records of the Circuit Court of Escambia County, Florida. Each of the letters is dated and noted not to have been read by the judge.

The piece, "Excerpt from Newspaper Report, 1998," comes from a *Pensacola News Journal* article written by reporter Sonja Lewis. The article "Judge ends 'dramatic' case with life sentence for man" appeared in *PNJ* on October 2, 1998.

The lines "a girl is born/ like a little bird opening its wing" are from Besmilr Brigham's poem "tell our daughters," published in *Cries of the Spirit*, edited by Marilyn Sewell (Boston: Beacon Press, 1991).

The lines "You do not do, you do not do/ Any more, black shoe" are from Sylvia Plath's poem "Daddy," which appears in *Ariel* (New York: Harper & Row, 1965).

The lines "Everyone in me is a bird./ I am beating all of my wings" are from Anne Sexton's "In Celebration of My Uterus," which appears in *The Complete Poems* of Anne Sexton (Boston: Mariner Books, 1981).

Acknowledgments

Versions of the poems in this book first appeared in the following publications:

Birmingham Poetry Review: "Portrait of My Father Eating Ice Cream . . . ," "Bullets in the Jewelry Box," and "Forsaking Our Pearls"
Black Warrior Review: "What Words"
Blue Fifth Review: "Lament," "In Celebration of Fifteen Years," and "A New Being"
Central Park: "Where I Have Been"
Chickenpinata: "Julie Holds a Hummingbird," "Crocus," and "Shopping List"
FutureCycle 2011: "Father Sends His Combat Medals in a Padded Brown Mailer, 1988" and "Portrait of Father Being Sentenced"
Girls with Insurance: "Interrogation"
Kennesaw Review: "Body of a Lunatic" and "A Taste of Ashes"
Peeks and Valley: "Rough with Each Other"
Prairie Schooner: "Bluebeard's Daughter" and "Persephone Lost"
Prick of the Spindle: "Minotaur Considered" and "Burqa, the Right Word for Grief"
Rio Grande Review: "How it Goes On"

Many of the poems in this collection also appeared in the chapbook, *Narcissistic Injury,* published by Pudding House in 2009.

Cover photo, "Crashed Dreams," by Elena Helfrecht of Apokryphia Art (apokryphiaart.jimdo.com)

Cover and book design by Diane Kistner (dkistner@futurecycle.org)

Photo of the author by Jon Brooks

Text, titling, and cover type: Chaparral Pro

www.ingramcontent.com/pod-product-compliance
Lightning Source LLC
Chambersburg PA
CBHW070007100426
42741CB00012B/3144